AFRICAN DESIGNS OF THE GUINEA COAST

CAREN CARAWAY

Stemmer House
PUBLISHERS, INC.
Owings Mills, Maryland

INTRODUCTION

Odomankoma
Created the thing.
Borebore (the Architect)
Created the thing.
He created what?
He created the Court-Cryer,
He created the Poet-Drummer,
He created Touch-and Die
As principals.

Drum song from *A Treasury of African Folklore* by Harold Courlander
Crown Publishers, Inc., N.Y., © 1975

ODOMANKOMA, THE SUPREME DIETY of the Ashanti, was the creative force that manifested the physical universe. He also created the Court-Cryer who represents universal order, the Poet-Drummer, symbolic of knowledge and tradition, and Touch-and Die, who is death. Humans consider Odomankoma too remote to be directly addressed so they supplicate him through other means such as the spirits of dead ancestors.

This is a common practice for many of the people who inhabit the Guinea Coast, which is mainly a belt of rain forest near the equator in west Africa. It is primarily low-lying and fertile, with considerable regions of savannah. The savannah provided an easier life and favored the formation of large kingdoms founded by bands of mounted warriors. The aristocracy of kings and court nobles gained social prestige with the display of wealth expressed with secular arts.

In the dense forest, life was more difficult and it led to the development of powerful secret societies for which art served religion. An abundance of wood, leaves, bark, fibers, clay, stone, bone, ivory, iron and gold was used in the manufacture of objects which functioned as an important part of daily life. Iron had been used for 2000 years, and axes and knives forged from it were used to carve masks and figures from single pieces of wood. Artists begged forgiveness from the spirit of the tree for the pain they caused when cutting the needed wood. Most African artists are unknown; many were farmers unless they lived in cultures where guilds received royal patronage. Most of their creations have been destroyed by a hot, humid climate unsuitable for the preservation of wooden objects. But the art that remains serves as a magnificent historic record of the many cultures that inhabited the Guinea Coast.

The fierce warriors of the FON established a powerful kingdom in southern Dahomey from the 17th to the end of the 19th centuries. The sacral king resided in the fortified city of Abomey. Protected by armed amazons and served by hundreds of women and slaves, kings were occasionally subjected to ritual killing. The lucrative sale of captives to the slave trade provided great power and wealth, some of which was used to create splendid secular items for the king and his court. The palace pillars, doors and thrones were decorated with sculptures, the inner walls were hung with bright appliques, and the outer walls were covered with clay relief tablets depicting battle scenes. The Fon made the largest forged iron sculpture in Africa. For a time the king monopolized the family guilds that produced textiles, silver and brass founding. The carving of wood and calabashes were the only crafts available to ordinary people. Wood was carved into wood trays and cups, charms and combs, staffs and stools. Calabashes were carved with stylized figures which represented words in a riddle or proverb.

Some of the art of Togo is related to ancient cultures such as the Abron, the first of the forest kingdoms in

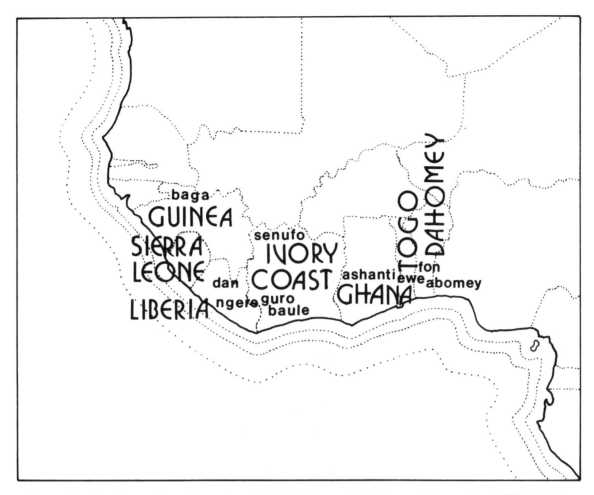

Ghana. Akan immigrants from the west established small states in the forest of Ghana about 1600 A.D. In the late 17th and early 18th centuries, the ASHANTI used the superiority of their firearms to create a powerful military federation under the leadership of their first king, who received divine sanction when, according to legend, a golden stool fell from heaven upon his knees during a thunderstorm. The stool was considered to contain the soul of the Ashanti people and the strength of the nation. On the coast, the Ashanti extensively traded gold and slaves to the Europeans and maintained a splendid capital, Kumasi, located at the center of a thickly forested plateau.

Ghana has some of the richest gold mines in the world, and gold was found abundantly in shallow rivers and on coastal shores. It was considered to be symbolic of the sun and bearer of the soul power of the Ashanti. Gold dust was the universal currency. It was measured with the use of brass weights beautifully made in numerous forms. The king's weights were heavier, thus imposing an automatic tax. The king was representative of the sun and was all-powerful. Neither the king nor the golden stool was allowed to touch the ground. Art was courtly and secular, not religious, despite the fact that there was a pantheon of gods. The king and nobility wore small golden masks, heads and animals cast by a highly developed lost wax process. They wore magnificent textiles of cotton and silk. Personally designed kente cloth was woven in long narrow strips, then sewn together. Adinkra cloth was imprinted with stamps carved from calabashes. Such cloth could be read by those who knew the meanings of the patterns. It is said the Ashanti obtained the art of cloth printing when they killed a king in battle who was wearing the cloth. State swords made of metal were symbolic of the king's power and metal founders were considered upper aristocracy. The Ashanti did not believe in ancestor figures and the gods were not represented by images. They were basically maskless because of the absence of puberty ceremonies and sacred rituals. Wood sculpture was limited to fertility figures carried by women and girls. And there were household items such as wooden combs, loom pulleys, game boards, drums and human figures. Brass soul containers, believed to store up the power of dead souls, were offered sacrifices and were filled with gold, ornaments and cowries shells, and placed with the owner at time of death.

The SENUFO are a group of closely related tribes of northern Ivory Coast and southeast Mali, who speak four distinct languages. They are peaceful agriculturalists, whose women plant corn and millet on farms clustered around villages on the fertile rainy savannah. They claim to have migrated from the north 200 or 300 years ago. The Lo or Poro society governs their entire social and religious life. Men are grouped in three ranks according to age and may enter the next rank every seven years after a period of testing. Women have their own secret shrine and ceremonies. Senufo carvers belong to an old caste of smiths with a feared secret society of their own. They make all cult figures such as rhythm-beating statues—which play an important role at burials—various figures, carved doors and sacred drums. There are different categories of masks. The fantastic and terrifying helmet masks are created from powerful, symbolic animal elements and represent demonic bush spirits. When they conduct witch hunts at funerals and festivals women are not allowed to be present. Sometimes they are used as firesplitting masks, in which a tinder is placed between the jaws and set on fire as the masked, costumed figure jumps and bellows, blowing sparks out of the mouth. The face mask is of gentler form but represents the dreaded force of a dead man. The Poro society keeps its cult objects in a sacred grove which no stranger may enter under pain of death.

The GURO inhabit the center of the Ivory Coast. Their life is dominated by secret societies. Sculpted figures were rarely found, masks were their principle form of art. Representing human faces and animal heads, the masks were used for burials and to exorcise evil sorcerers.

The BAULE separated from the Ashanti about 1730, and under the leadership of an Ashanti queen, who sacrificed her little son to appease the spirits of a flooding river, migrated to the Ivory Coast where they founded a kingdom east of the Guro. They retained some Ashanti traditions and the arts of creating fabrics, wooden stools, sword handles and cast brass weights for measuring gold dust. They acquired carving and the use of masks from the Guro. The masks were generally flat and of two kinds, human faces and animal heads. Some masks represented mythic gods who averted evil and devoured witches at night. The Baule also carved two types of carefully finished human figures, dolls and ancestor statues. They believed the soul left the body after death and wandered the village, seeking a home. It was invited to inhabit a statue specially made for it, and in turn they received help and comfort from it in matters of fertility, agriculture and personal well-being and prosperity. Masters of bronze and gold, the Baule made sumptuous jewelry and gold items for personal adornment, as well as household objects such as loom pulleys, oracle containers and ointment pots.

The DAN are savannah tribes who migrated from the north 300 years ago to northern Liberia and the western Ivory Coast. Powerful secret societies dominate their cultural and religious life. Masks play a role in almost all social and religious events, but are of prime importance in the function of secret societies. The Dan believe earth life is ruled by an omnipotent being too remote for direct communication. An ancestral spirit, who is thought to reside with its terrestrial personality in a supernatural sphere, is used as an intercessor by means of a mask. Men used them to help control life and the environment. Each mask represents a spirit or divinity and each has its own name. A mask accumulates power with age and the sacrifices made to it, and its power determines how it is used in a higher or lower degree of the secret society. Masks of highest rank act as peace- and law-makers. War masks required the sacrifice of prisoners. Some protect pregnant women, babies and boys, twins and travelers. Others control thunder and lightning, cure illness, discover thieves and participate in circumcision ceremonies and burials. Only men were allowed to possess a mask and the highest form of sacrifice to a mask occurred when the owner killed his eldest son.

The NGERE are forest farmers in the western Ivory Coast and northern Liberia. They resemble the Dan in many ways. The Poro, the men's secret society, and the Sande, the women's association, taught boys and girls the duties of adulthood and conducted initiation ceremonies that included circumcision for the boys and excision for the girls. Smaller societies were concerned with politics, economics, medicine and morals. They used many different kinds of masks, but the Ngere masks were generally more grotesque, less naturalistic and extraordinarily powerful.

The BAGA live close to the sea in the swampy coastal region of Guinea. They themselves say that they migrated from an area near the source of the Niger. Most villages have since become Moslemized. The men fish and tend kola and palm trees, the women grow rice. Inheritance is matrilineal. There is obligatory marriage between a husband's brothers and his wife's sisters, and between a widow and her husband's younger brother or nephew. The people's lives are dominated by the powerful Simo secret society, which has social, political and religious authority. It is concerned with birth, circumcision and death, the three most important events of Baga life. The society has a system of degrees, a secret language and cult secrets, and it conducts rituals of isolation, initiation, circumcision and tatooing. It also promotes fertility of humans, animals and the earth. It determines the use of ritual implements, ceremonial drums and masks, which are frequently decorated with round-headed brass nails and worn with a fiber costume. Baga masks are the most massive of sub-Saharan Africa.

C.C.

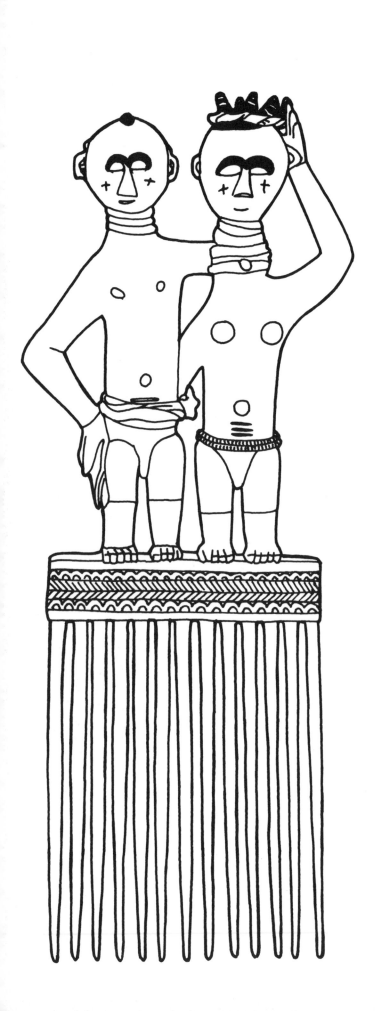
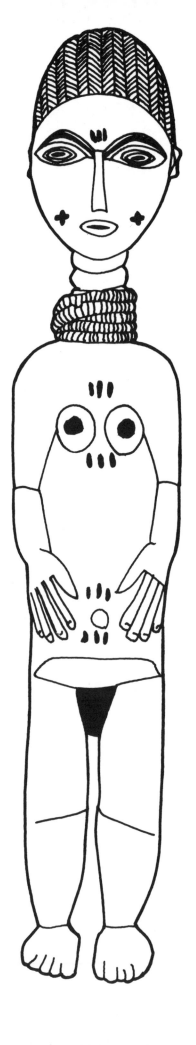

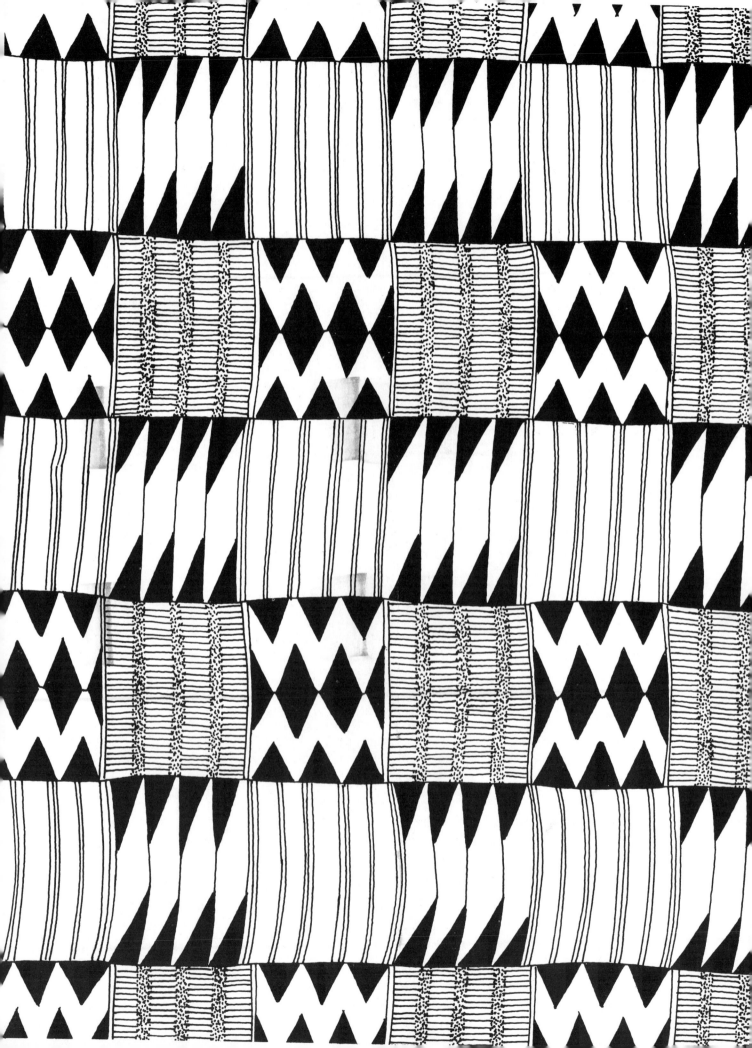

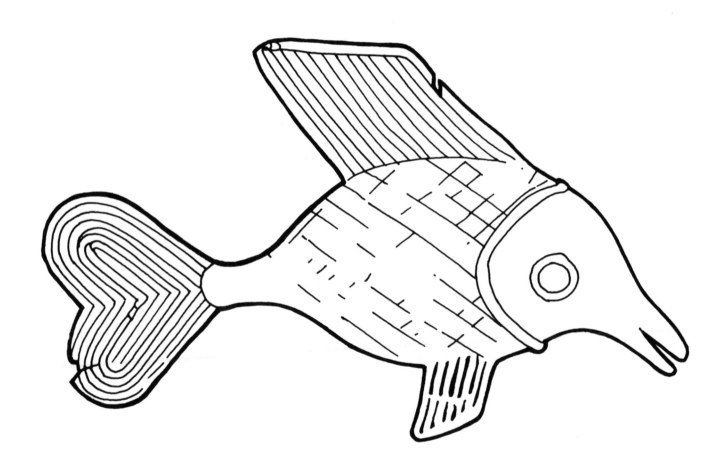

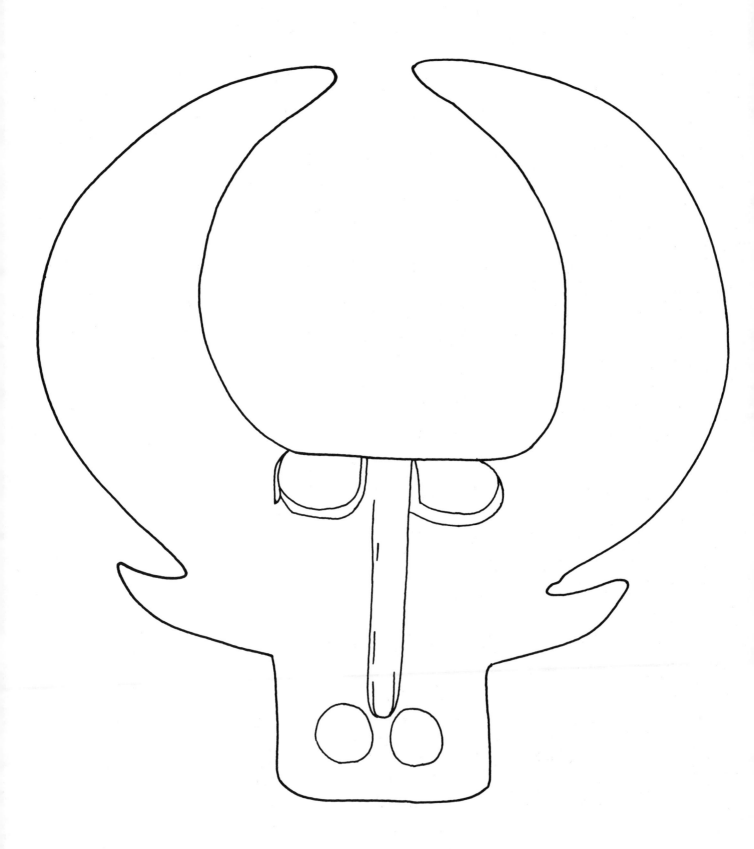

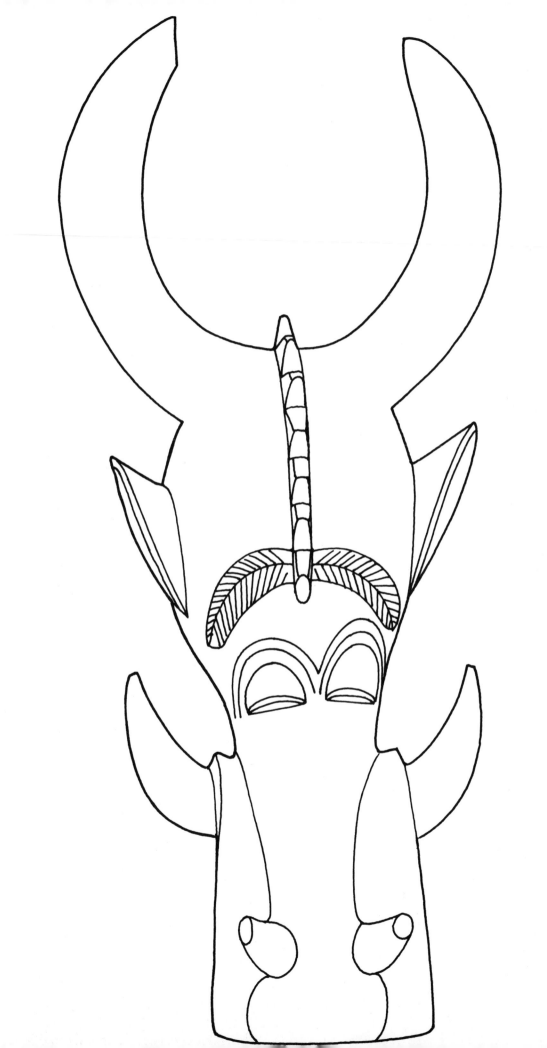

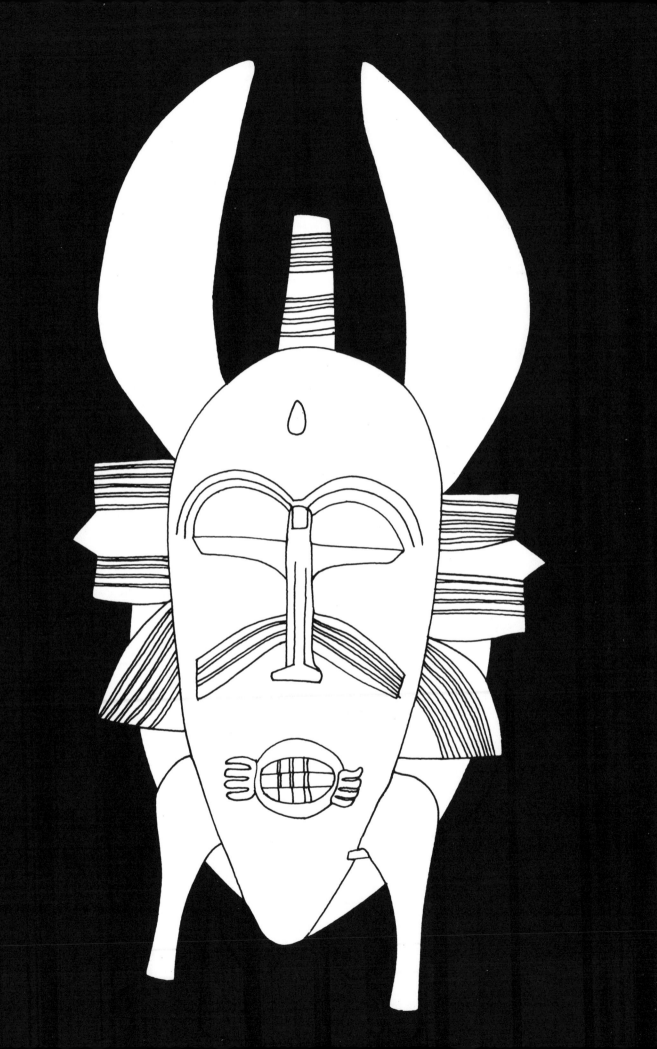

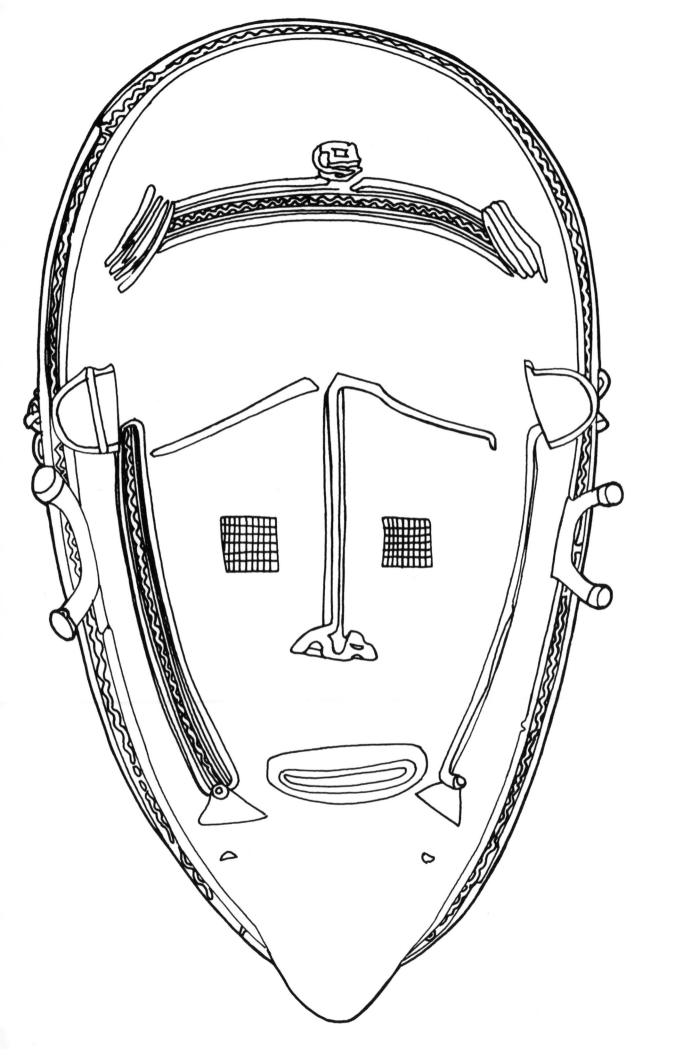

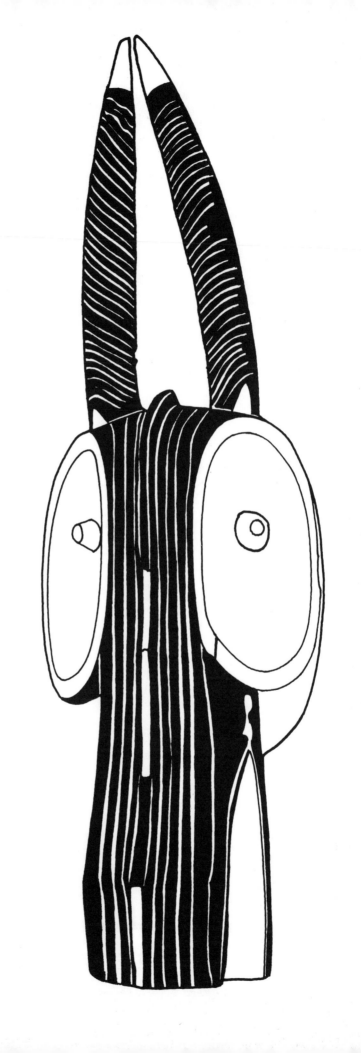

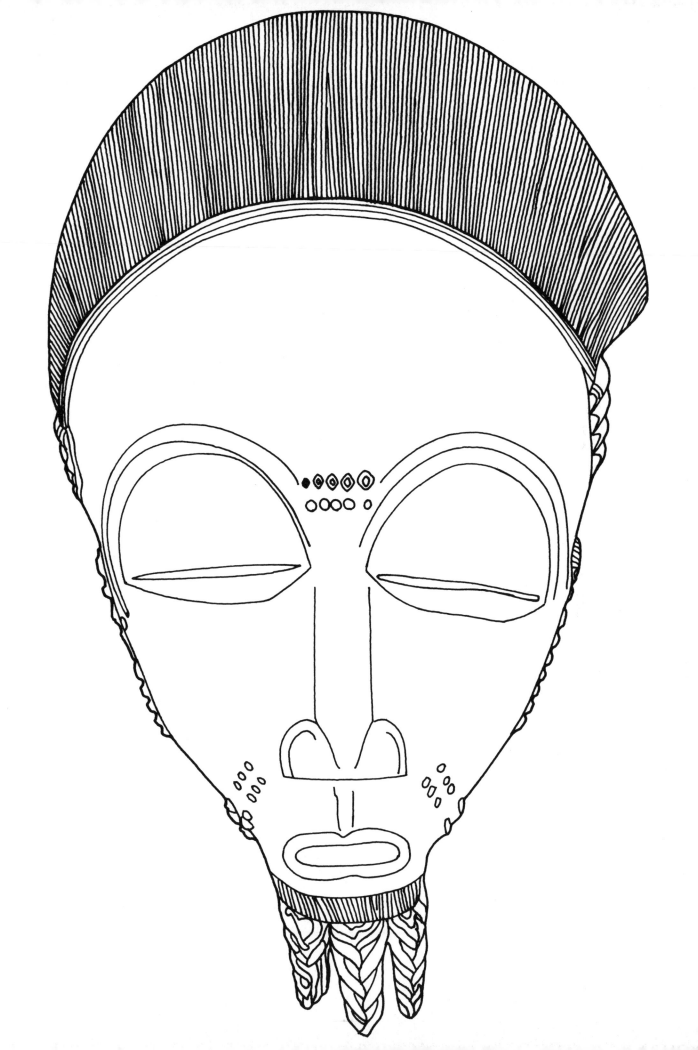

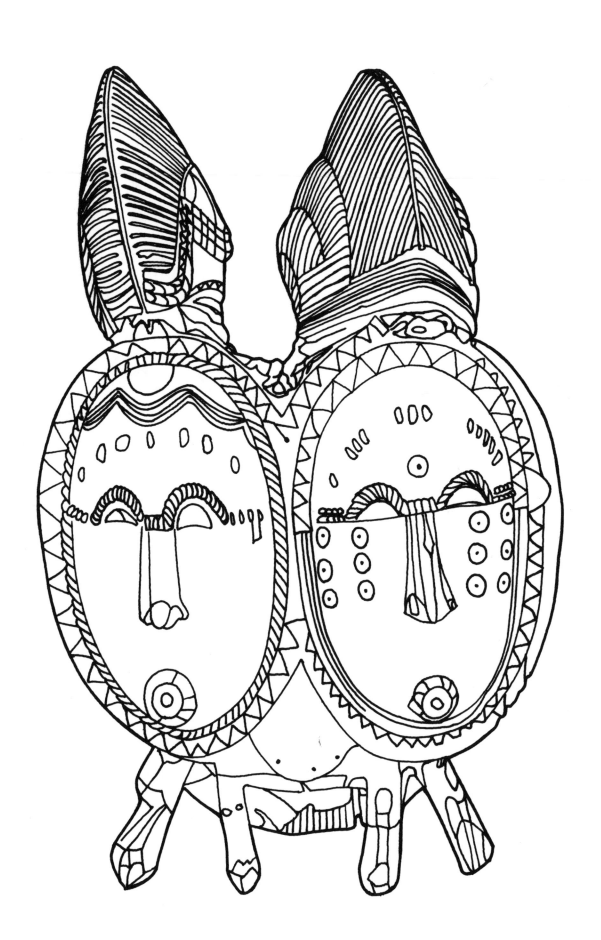

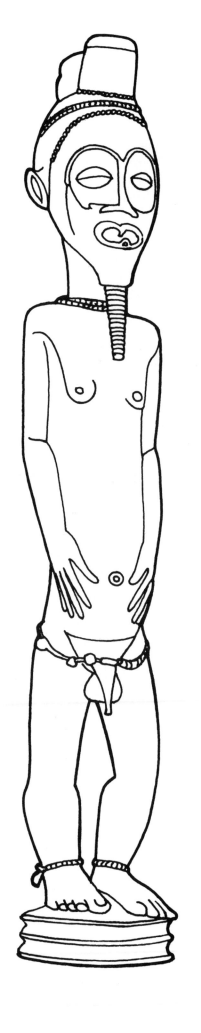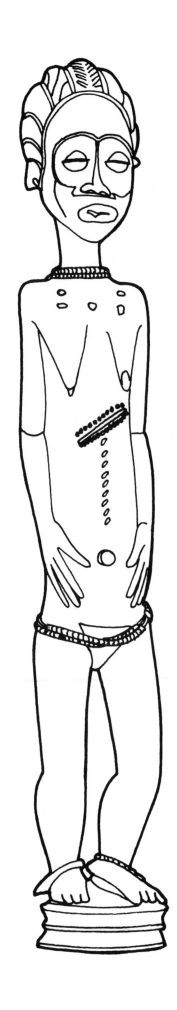

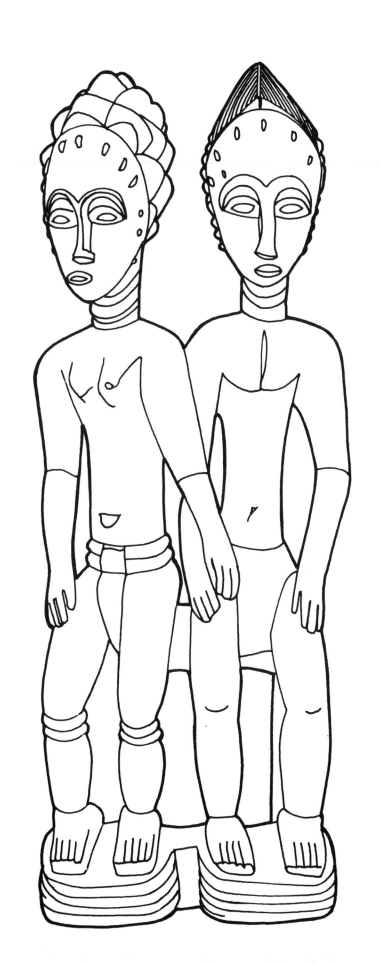

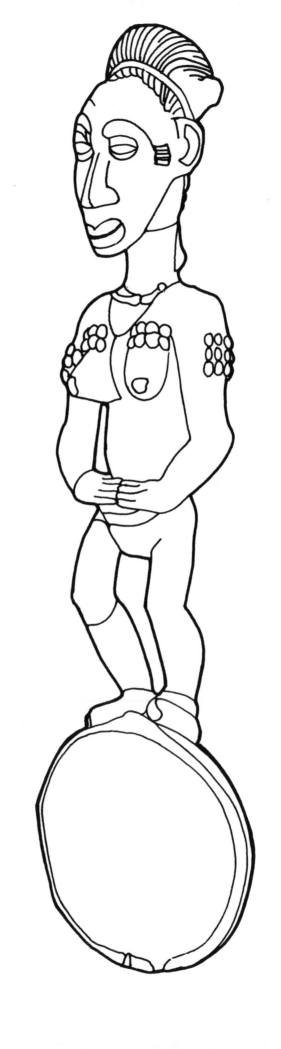

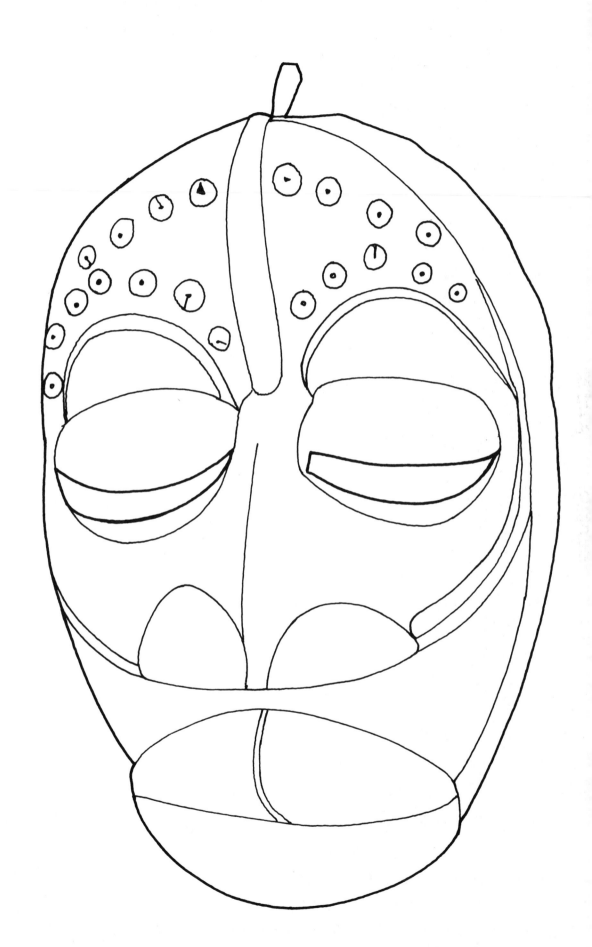

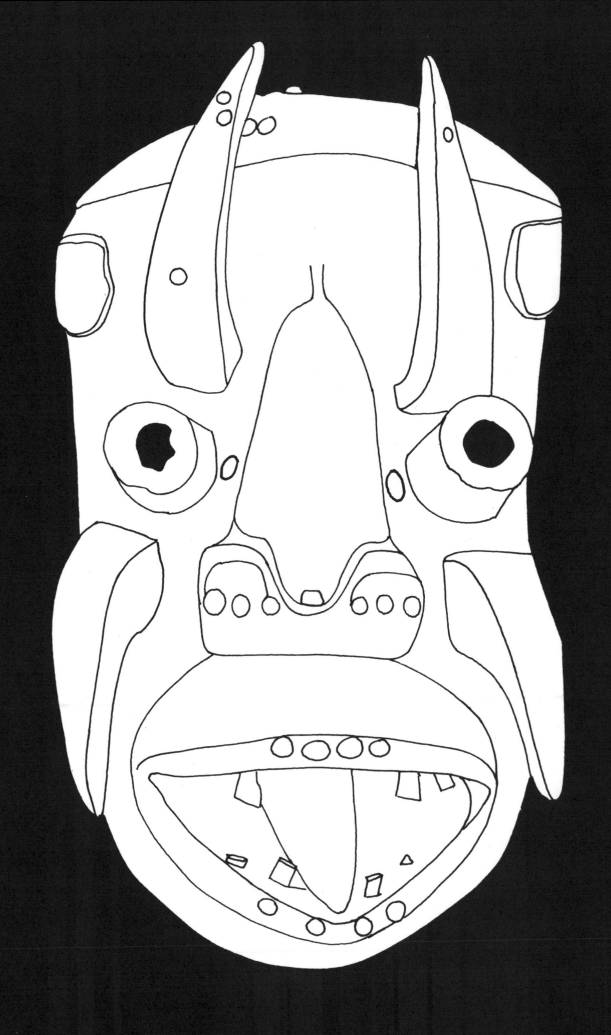

For Phyllis Walker Hodgson

who walked through the valley of the shadow of death several times
and emerged to say, "Welcome to the workshop of Life!"

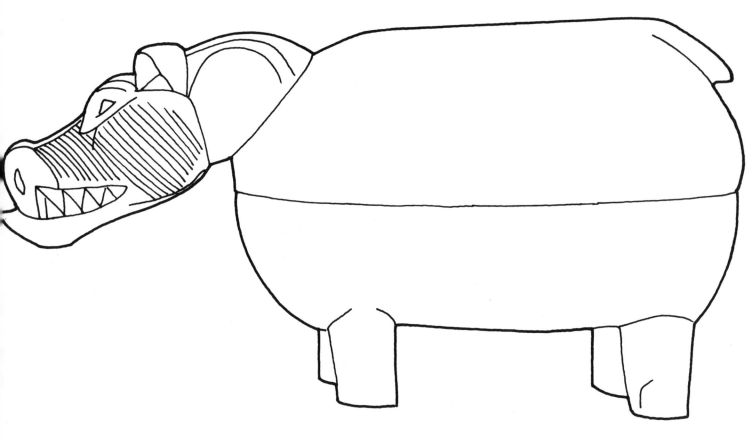

Designed by Barbara Holdridge
Composed in Times Roman by Brown Composition, Inc.,
    Baltimore, Maryland
Printed on 75-pound Williamsburg Offset paper and bound by
    BookCrafters, Fredericksburg, Virginia
Covers color-separated by Sun Crown, Washington, D.C.